Behind Media

Music

Sally Morgan
and Pauline Lalor

Heinemann

D1077833

www.heinemann.co.uk/library
Visit our website to find out more information about **Heinemann Library** books.

To order:
☎ Phone 44 (0) 1865 888066
📄 Send a fax to 44 (0) 1865 314091
💻 Visit the Heinemann Bookshop at www.heinemann.co.uk/library to browse our catalogue and order online.

First published in Great Britain by Heinemann Library, Halley Court, Jordan Hill, Oxford, OX2 8EJ,
a division of Reed Educational and Professional Publishing Ltd.
Heinemann is a registered trademark of Reed Educational and Professional Publishing Ltd.

OXFORD MELBOURNE AUCKLAND
JOHANNESBURG BLANTYRE GABORONE
IBADAN PORTSMOUTH NH (USA) CHICAGO

Designed by Paul Davies and Associates
Originated by Ambassador Litho Ltd.
Printed in Hong Kong/China

ISBN 0 431 11461 7 (hardback)   ISBN 0 431 11466 8 (paperback)
06 05 04 03 02   06 05 04 03 02
10 9 8 7 6 5 4 3 2 1   10 9 8 7 6 5 4 3 2

British Library Cataloguing in Publication Data

Morgan, Sally; Lalor, Pauline
  Music. - (Behind Media)
  1.Music - Juvenile literature
  I.Title
  780

Acknowledgements

Pauline Lalor wishes to dedicate this book in loving memory of her granddaughter, Leila.

The Publisher would like to thank the following for permission to reproduce photographs: Trevor Clifford: pp6, 7, 28, 31, 35, 36, 41; Corbis: pp14, 25, Nubar Alexanian p22, Henry Diltz p38, Jim Sugar p24; European Press Agency: p17; Hipenosis Design Co/Mike Prior/Redferns: p34; NME/Billboard/Recovery/Melody Maker/Esky/Trevor Clifford: p41; Press Association/Neil Munns: p40; © Queen Productions Ltd: p30; Redferns: Richie Aaron p10, Michael Ochs Archives pp5, 9, 12, Paul Bergan p11, Suzi Gibbons p21, Mick Hutson pp8, 18, 23, 26, 44, Jm International p5, Simon King p27, Michel Linssen p20; Rex Features: p45, Nils Jorgensen p42, Brian Moody p19, Andrew Murray p29, Brian Rasic p5; SPL: Maximilian Stock Ltd. p32, Philippe Plailly/Eurelios p32; Stone/Getty: p43.

Cover photograph reproduced with permission of Redferns.

Our thanks to Mike Collins for his comments in the preparation of this book.

Every effort has been made to contact copyright holders of any material reproduced in this book.
Any omissions will be rectified in subsequent printings if notice is given to the Publisher.

Contents

Fifty Years of Popular Music

Getting a Contract

Recording the Music

Burning the CD

Making a Hit

Any words appearing in the text in bold, **like this**, are explained in the Glossary.

Fifty Years of Popular Music

Making music

The last 50 years have seen many changes in the music industry. When the recording business began, musicians could 'cut a record' in a morning. The singer would hear the song on the piano, be handed the words, the red light would go on, the orchestra begin to play and the recording would begin! Nowadays, the recording process is far more complex. Once, making a record was just one of the jobs musicians undertook, but now it has become the major concern for many 'would-be' stars. This book looks at some of the facets of this fascinating and frustrating business, showing the processes and people involved in making a music **CD**.

A turning point

The thread running through all the changes in the industry is the fact that people love making and listening to music. The image and the music style might change, but **albums** and **singles** are selling better than ever. The turning point for music as we know it today was the arrival of rock and roll towards the end of the 1950s. Its arrival revolutionized popular music. With the 1960s came 'flower power' and even more emphasis on the voice of the young, much of this reflected in the music. The most important group of the decade was The Beatles, who attracted a young and impressionable audience. Their influence is still felt today, 30 years after they split up. By the 1970s, 'image' had become important and the incredibly theatrical glam rock performers took this to the extreme. This was followed by the punk rock music explosion – a reaction to the sophisticated sounds of the disco music of the 1970s. It was meant to shock and opened the door to many bands like the Sex Pistols in the UK and MC5 in the USA. In total contrast, reggae also became popular. Here, the rhythms and instruments showed influences from Jamaica, Africa and America.

The arrival of synthesized music

The 1980s were a rich decade for music and the pop audience was even bigger. Bands such as the Australian INXS filled huge world sports stadia, presenting a range of styles from rock and roll to pop to dance. But big changes were afoot, when bands such as Spandau Ballet and Depeche Mode moved away from traditional instruments and started to experiment with **synthesizers**, drum machines and new recording techniques to produce highly original 'synth pop'. By the late 1980s, house music, which used **samplers** and drum machines, and garage music had both arrived on the scene. Dance music really came into its own and presented a very different face of pop music as it was played in clubs from albums by a DJ, with no live band – and it seems it is here to stay. The 1980s also saw the arrival of the first music CDs in the shops. One of the first artists to use this new medium was Michael Jackson in 1982 when he released his album *Thriller* – the largest selling album of all time. The singles **charts** of the 1990s were dominated by the 'designer' bands that are still popular today, such as Boyzone, Take That, Westlife and The Spice Girls. These bands were formed for the express purpose of recording music that would appeal to the younger market.

Today, it is common to see a wide range of musicians in the charts. Featured here are Macy Gray, a top-selling artist of recent years, Tom Jones who first had hits in the 1960s and Bob Marley whose albums are still selling many years after his death.

Music media

The delivery of music has changed as much as the style of the music itself. During much of the 20th century, music was recorded on to **vinyl** records that were played on a record player. Vinyl records stored music as a long, shallow groove that spiralled around the disc. Up until the 1950s, records had one song on each side and were played at 78 revolutions per minute (rpm). By the start of the 1950s, the real age of vinyl had begun with long-playing **albums** (LPs). In these, the grooves carrying the sound were made finer and packed closer together and the speed of rotation was reduced to 33 rpm, so that more vibrations were recorded in the same length of grooves. Unfortunately, vinyl is a relatively soft material so the grooves were easily damaged. LPs were large so that they could accommodate the long length of grooves, but they warped easily and this distorted the sound.

The obvious disadvantage of the record player and the large reel-to-reel tape machines of the 1960s was that they were not portable and music could only be listened to at home. By the 1970s, small audio cassettes had become very popular and many young people owned personal stereos. These were small enough to be carried in a pocket or on a belt, being just a little larger than the cassette itself. The music was listened to through headphones, so people could have their music wherever they went.

The most popular form of music medium today is the CD. Sales of CDs are increasing each year, with millions sold each week. It remains to be seen whether new media such as MP3, which can be delivered via the Internet, will affect CD sales.

Although CDs represent two-thirds of all sales, record companies also release singles and albums in a range of media, including the more traditional vinyl records and tapes. Newer media, such as mini-discs and DVDs, are seeing an increase in popularity.

The birth of the digital era

When the first compact discs, or **CDs**, arrived in 1982, another revolution had begun. CDs quickly replaced vinyl records as they produced better quality sound. The needle of the record player was replaced by a **laser**, so wear and tear during play became a thing of the past. Sales steadily increased and in 1994 CDs outsold cassettes for the first time. Now, approximately 2.4 billion CDs are sold each year and they represent two-thirds of all album sales. During the late 1990s, new storage media such as **mini-discs** and **DVDs** (digital versatile – or video – discs) arrived in the shops. The Internet is also playing an increasingly important role in providing a listening post for music and it is clearly going to be one of the most important music sources of the future. Today, record companies have to issue an album in a range of different media.

The recipe for success

The ultimate dream of nearly every singer and musician is to make it big and be a star! A recording **contract** is the great ambition, and many aspiring stars feel they have begun to climb the ladder of success once they have achieved this. However, they may be in for disappointment if they don't appreciate all the hard work that goes into even getting a foot in the door. It is vital to do the necessary background work to ensure that a really good recording deal is achieved.

*Kylie Minogue was a well-known Australian soap star before she turned to singing. A fortuitous meeting with the music producer, Pete Waterman, led to her first hit song with the catchy **lyric** 'I should be so lucky'.*

What the record company is looking for

Go into any music shop and you will find as many different types of music on sale as there are potential buyers. Specialized radio stations and clubs promote varying styles, while retailers cater for everyone. People's tastes range from classical music, musicals or movie scores to jazz, folk, country or world music, from soul, blues or rock to pop, dance or Brit pop. There are many other variations and many people like several different kinds of music.

In pure musical terms, what makes a hit record changes from year to year. A hit record, or essentially a hit **single**, is the result of more than a brilliant voice, a new dance craze, or being a sex symbol. The most important single ingredient of a hit record is the song.

Unless a **talent scout** has seen a band live and the record company is already interested in it, it is up to the musicians to convince the record company of their talent and potential for success. The record company will be looking for ability in terms of the music and lyrics, not necessarily a particular style. Most of the major record companies have different **labels**, specializing in different styles of music, so they can direct the musicians to the right label. Musicians can also approach the independent labels ('indies') that tend to specialize in certain types of music.

As well as ability, bands must have the right image for the time. Their face has got to 'fit' so that the record-buying public can relate to them. They will be seen live, on video, television and the Internet, and their lives and opinions will be expressed in all areas of the media.

New trends in music are usually picked up and encouraged by the independent and specialist labels and later, if the 'new' music begins to attract general attention, the major labels will move in. However, all record company signings include an element of timing and luck!

First impressions

Nowadays, 'demo CDs' are important. These are demonstration CDs containing a few songs recorded by the aspiring band. They have to be as near to professional quality as possible. Demos are sent to the A&R department of a record company, where people are employed to listen to them all and decide if an artist is to be signed up. They hear a lot of demos each day, so it is important that a new band creates a good first impression. Also, a good recording shows that the band has confidence in itself. The days when a home-produced audio cassette would suffice are long gone. It is essential to submit a well-produced CD.

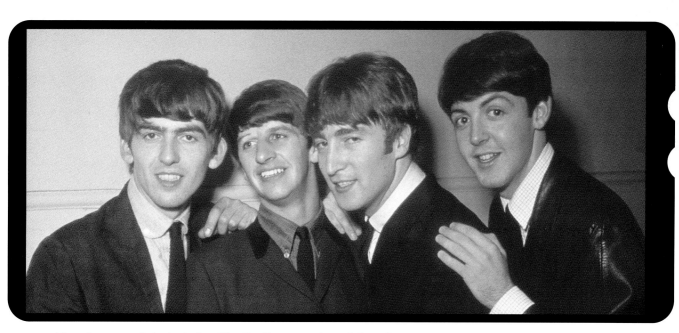

Many famous artists, including The Beatles, were turned down by very knowledgeable, successful people in the music business before finally being signed up. Today, everyone knows how their image came to be synonymous with the 1960s!

Race in the music industry

The music industry seems to be an area where all races, colours and cultures are accepted. Many bands have a complete racial mix and are the richer for it. There is a fast-growing Asian pop music scene nowadays and there have always been many famous black musicians, particularly in the field of jazz, blues, soul and of course reggae. Most people know of Jimi Hendrix and Bob Marley, both now dead. Also, the Motown artists include many famous black singers, such as Stevie Wonder and Diana Ross.

Inspiration and perspiration

O bviously one of the most important aspects in obtaining a record deal is the songs that the band performs. In the past, songwriting performers were rare, but nowadays the singer-songwriter is much more common. Although a band does not need to write its own material, songwriting ability is a definite plus.

Songwriting

It has been said that songwriting is 'ten per cent inspiration and ninety per cent perspiration'! It is both an art and a craft, and the best way to improve is to keep at it. The difference between a **lyric** and a poem, according to successful American lyricist Sammy Cahn, is that a poem is meant 'for the eye' and a lyric 'for the ear'. A great lyric is one that helps a song to become a hit. What is important is that the lyric fits the music.

The members of a band need to have a style that is individual, but is also one which their audience will relate to. The subject of a song must reflect the times, too, so that listeners can identify with it. A unique sound and songwriting ability are the elements that interest a record company and can make the difference between being signed up or not.

Many band members do not write songs themselves, but they contribute to the final version during jamming sessions. During a session, different arrangements are tried out and the song evolves.

The making of a song

Bands vary enormously in their approach to songwriting. Traditionally, songwriting involved someone writing lyrics and putting some chords on a guitar or keyboard. This, of course, is still often the way a song develops. Sometimes, a band will get together and just **jam** and a song will come out of the **session**. Rock bands still do this and possibly will continue to get much of their inspiration in this way. In a heavy rock band, it could be that the drummer plays around on the drums, the guitarist joins in, the bass player adds some bass runs and, once the lead singer has tried out a few lyrics, they find they have something with which they are all pleased. A song has been born.

Another method might be that the singer comes to rehearsal with some chords, a melody and the first verse of a song written and then the rest of the band will collaborate in finishing it off. Or perhaps, that same group may start with a title and an idea and will then actually write the song together. Sometimes, one of the band members comes in with an entire song with which all the band are happy and that will be the finished article.

It is extremely important that a band continues to produce new material all the time. The songwriter must have an urge to write continually, even if every song is not recorded. Record companies need to know that there will be a constant stream of new material.

Often the main lyric-writer in a band is the lead singer because he or she is the one who has to identify with the subject of the song. However, this is not always the case. In Oasis, Noel Gallagher has written songs, which are sung by his brother Liam.

The importance of
a manager

So you have formed your own band, you write your own **lyrics**, you think you know quite a bit about the music business and you have found out what the record companies are looking for. But what about a **manager**?

Do you need a manager?

Most successful musicians and singers rely on their manager to take care of the business side of band life, leaving them free to perform, write material and record. It is perfectly possible for a band to manage itself. Semi-professional musicians or singers, and even some professional ones, can exist for years without a manager, but most of the really successful bands have one.

A manager can usually argue the case for the band more easily than the band can on its own. But a manager's true value is revealed after the band has obtained a record deal. It is at this stage that the hard-earned skill of diplomacy and the extracting of favours really come into play.

The good relationship between Elvis Presley and his manager Colonel Tom Parker seemed to be one of the key ingredients in Elvis' success. Colonel Parker is reported to have said, 'When I first knew Elvis he had a million dollars worth of talent. Now he has a million dollars.'

On the job

A manager looks after the band, taking care of everything except writing and making the music. He or she handles the business side of the band's career, using his or her contacts in the music business actively to promote the band, by booking and supervising gigs and tours and getting publicity and press coverage. The manager is responsible for setting up a recording contract, negotiating **royalty** payments and liaising with lawyers, accountants, journalists and record company **A&R** departments. A good manager can turn their hand to any job, at any time of the day or night.

How do you choose a manager?

The first essential for a manager is commitment and a genuine interest in the band and its music. Eventually though, the band members may be approached by a big management company who will ask them to sign a **contract** that puts the band completely in the company's hands for a number of years. Good management can really 'make' a band's career, but bad management can 'break' it.

Management contracts

Ideally, a band will seek specialist professional legal advice before it signs up with a manager. The agreement should at least include a provision for the manager to advance and promote the band's career and ensure that all money payable to the band is collected and properly accounted for. The manager will want to ensure that the deal is exclusive – that is, the band is not signed to any other management – and that the band will honour all contracts and not attempt to enter into any on its own. In return for all their business advice, managers take a **commission** from everything that the band earns. This is usually between fifteen and twenty per cent. So for every £100 earned by a band, the manager will take about £20.

Real life!

It may sound as if it is only the band that might get caught out in a relationship with a manager. However, there are many 'dumped' managers, who did not have a proper contract with their band, who have put in all the hard work, not to mention the money, and have been left behind when the band became big. Many friends who start off managing a small band are only too pleased when the band becomes noticed by important people, who can more effectively manage an up-and-coming band's career, but there are others who have experienced painful rejection.

Female artists in the music world

The pop music world has always been male dominated, despite an enormous amount of female talent. The management side of the industry has been almost exclusively male. Some of the first girl bands had their songs written for them by men! Some established artists, including Madonna and Tina Turner, have been managing their own careers for many years, but it has been encouraging to see the rise of 'girl power' with the success of The Spice Girls, who also control their own careers. Now, there are many popular new female artists such as Britney Spears and Shania Twain.

Agents, promoters and the rest!

Part of the **manager's** job is to put in place a back-up team to ensure the success of the band. He or she must put the band in touch with an **agent** to get bookings and arrange tours, and search for **promoters** to finance **gigs** and tours.

The agent

The main role of the agent is to obtain work for the band. Agents are often criticized for apparently doing nothing but living off 'their' acts, as they usually do not invest any money in the developing bands with whom they work. Agents make their money by taking a percentage of the fees that they negotiate on behalf of a band for a live performance. They usually expect about ten per cent of live fees as a **commission** and expect to have a **contract** that lasts one to five years. Some agents work with a wide range of musicians, whilst others specialize in particular kinds of acts. They are often good talent spotters, picking out new acts at live gigs. They can also be approached by individual bands, who supply them with **demos**, in much the same way as bands approach record companies in order to get a record deal.

The promoter

Promoters actually finance gigs and tours, either by approaching a band direct or by negotiating a band's fee via their agent or manager. It is the promoters who organize and run live shows and whose money is at risk. They are of necessity businessmen or women and may, or may not, have a genuine interest in music.

On a small scale, there are the promoters who are tied to a specific venue, such as a club or a pub. They may be full-time bookers or managers employed by the licensee of the venue, or they may be independent individuals who have an arrangement with the proprietor of the venue where they promote frequently. These are the promoters that bands meet in the early stages of their career and who book bands through personal taste or because they believe they are up-and-coming acts.

Most of the major promoters are based in the big cities. At this level, promoters deal almost exclusively through agents when putting together individual dates or tours. They hear about interesting new acts through the record companies and from agents, journalists, lawyers and the managers of the concert halls they regularly use. They search mainly for bands with record deals and preferably good record sales. At the mega-star level, there are promoters who book concert halls or work exclusively at stadia and festivals.

Some of the largest venues in the world can hold tens of thousands of people. The largest audiences are seen at open air venues such as this one in California in the USA. It is only the top-selling bands, with a large following, that can sell enough tickets to fill these venues on their own.

On the job

A successful agent is one who keeps a band busy all year. The agent and manager will hold discussions about the band's record release schedule, the type of performance that the band is capable of putting on, the amount of money they need to earn to cover their touring costs and their future hopes. Armed with this information, the agent contacts venues and promoters to secure bookings for the band. The agent is responsible for all the negotiation involving the performance contract and fees and will make all the arrangements with the venue. He or she may also collect money owed to the band.

Recording contracts – what does the band want?

Suddenly it all seems a bit more complicated than just forming a band, writing some songs and going for a record deal. There seem to be a lot of people involved in the process, all of them taking their cut of any money that the band make. Bands have to be very careful that they are not taken advantage of.

There are many stories of famous bands who have lost the rights to their own recorded songs. The best advice for a band is always to seek professional legal advice before agreeing to anything. A band and its management want to get the best deal for the good of the band. Conversely, the record company needs to be sure that it is going to be profitable for it to finance a particular musical act. The company must protect its own interests too.

Music and the law

The vast majority of bands first become aware of the need for professional advice when they are presented with their first long-term **contract** and are advised to consult a solicitor over its terms. The contractual and legal aspects of the music business have become increasingly complex and sophisticated. As a result, there are now many specialist music lawyers who work in the music industry. It is now the norm for **managers**, record companies, **publishers** and so on to insist that the bands whom they wish to contract should have the benefit of independent legal advice before signing.

What is copyright?

It is mainly through songwriting and/or composing that a musician can earn a decent living. A band could sell thousands of **albums**, but if it had not written any of the songs it would earn comparatively little. Songwriters need to protect the **copyright** of their songs. Copyright means, quite literally, the right to prevent other people copying an original work. There is no copyright in ideas. As far as musical compositions are concerned, the author is the person who first created them. This person is automatically able to control and collect the **royalties** arising from any use of the work. There is a different copyright made of the sound recording of the work. The sound recording is generally owned by the company who paid for the recording, that is, the record company. Copyright can be very confusing for people working in the music business if they do not grasp this distinction.

Under UK and Australian copyright law a songwriter does not have to do anything to copyright a song. Copyright protection automatically comes into existence as soon as an original musical work has been created – provided that it is written down or recorded in some way. In the USA, published works used to have to be registered to determine the ownership of copyright but it is now no longer compulsory.

One method that composers use to establish the date when a song came into existence, in case of dispute, is to send a copy of the work to themselves in a printed official registered envelope. They write the title of the work on the outside and when it arrives they attach the postal service receipt and keep it unopened in a safe place, with the postmark being evidence of when it was posted.

Loss of copyright

In the past, control of copyright was not seen as being very important, and many inexperienced artists lost control over the copyright of some of their most famous songs. One famous case was that of The Beatles. Much of the copyright of their early material is now in the ownership of Michael Jackson. He paid millions of dollars for the copyright and he receives royalty payments on these songs.

*The rise in popularity of MP3 websites, where people can **download** music tracks for free, has lead to record companies and bands taking action to protect their copyright. In 2000, a number of individuals, including Lars Ulrich, drummer of Metallic (left), testified before the US Senate Committee on Music on the Internet.*

Record companies

Record companies are responsible for producing the music **CDs** that are sold in shops around the world. These companies range from small independents that specialize in one type of music to huge multi-nationals that represent all types of bands and artists.

The recording contract at last!

Before any recording takes place, the record company will draw up a recording **contract** for the band. There is no such thing as a standard recording contract, but certain issues will need to be formalized:

✢ the term – the period during which a band is signed to its record company and all recording services are given exclusively to the company. There is usually an 'initial period' of perhaps twelve months and then several 'option periods'. A band has to negotiate to reduce the potential length of the term so that it will not be tied to the record company indefinitely, or so that it can renegotiate the deal if it becomes successful

✢ the band will be required to make a minimum number of recordings during the term

✢ the record company will expect to have absolute control over the type of music recorded

✢ time schedules for recording will have to be arranged

✢ agreement must be made regarding payment, usually **advances** being paid at the start of each contract period, triggered by the release of a **single** or by certain **chart** positions.

*Unlike many dance bands, Prodigy were noticed by a record company by doing a large number of **gigs**. They released their first record,* What Evil Lurks, *in February 1991. They supported this by doing non-stop gigs and were rewarded with sales of 7000 copies. Their second release, a single, reached number three in the UK charts. Their debut double **album**,* The Prodigy Experience, *was described as being the finest LP to come from the rave scene.*

What the record company expects

When signed up with one record company, it is not possible for a band to record with anybody else unless permission is first granted by the record company. It will be unable to re-record any of the songs that were recorded under the contract for a period of five years from the end of the contract. The band will be expected to belong to a professional musicians' association, such as Equity or the Musicians' Union. The band is also required to ensure that there are no previously unreleased recordings that could be released by someone else. If there are, the record company may require ownership of them. The record company will expect to use photographs and information about the lives of the band members for the sale and promotion of the songs.

The publisher

As well as a record company, a new band needs to find a **publisher**. A publisher will protect the **copyright** of a song on behalf of the songwriter. In the past, music publishers printed and sold sheet music in a similar way to those publishers dealing with books. They bought the world rights to a song for a small fee, and then took their income from the sales of the sheet music and the **royalties** paid when 'their' songs were performed on stage and screen. Now, though, it is the royalties earned from radio and TV broadcasts, live performances and the sales of recordings of their songs that provide their income. Publishers retain a share of the royalties earned by the songs on which they hold the copyright.

Many publishers actively search for songwriters whom they think could become commercially successful. They will then help them to develop their career, sometimes by funding a **demo** at their own cost and personally taking it round to the heads of **A&R** departments. Their aim is to get a recording contract or to get their artists' songs on the soundtracks to films and advertisements.

*In 1970, Richard Branson set up Virgin Records, a mail order supplier of pop records which expanded into a chain of shops. Virgin also had a record **label** and represented well-known artists such as Phil Collins, Heaven 17, Human League and Simple Minds. Richard Branson, with his 'unstuffy' style, presented a very human side to record company management.*

Recording the Music

Preparing to record

So at last a new band is ready to start recording. The first thing the record company will probably want the band to do is to go into a studio and make a **demo** of everything it has ever written. This will be followed by long discussions about which songs to release as **singles**, and a **producer** will be found. Many producers are linked to a particular studio, where they are familiar with the equipment and have developed a good working relationship with the **sound engineer**, so the choice of producer may determine the choice of studio.

The playing area of the studio is fitted with microphones. Here, each of the singers has a microphone to pick up the vocals. Headphones eliminate all the other sounds in the room and allow the singer to hear the backing track.

On the job

A producer is somebody who is experienced in the technical aspects of sound recording. They have a good knowledge of music and should be able to offer positive criticism without upsetting the band. They will help to select the band's material, choose the studio and engineer, direct the session and hire **session musicians** or backing singers when required. Their fee comes out of the band's **advance** from the record company or from future **royalties**.

The master recording studio

The moment of truth has come at last – the band is actually in the studio itself! Normally a recording studio is divided into at least two rooms, the soundproof playing area and the control room. The playing area might also be further divided to contain a vocal booth. Anything that will involve using a microphone must be recorded in the soundproof playing area to avoid **feedback** between the microphone and control room speakers and monitors. Microphones of varying shapes and sizes will be used for different items, such as drums, guitars, vocals and any instruments being played through amplifiers, usually referred to as 'amps'.

The control room is very much the nerve centre of any studio and this is where the engineer and the producer sit to record and direct the **session**. They can see what is going on in the playing area and can communicate with the performers. Whereas the producer is responsible for 'directing' the performers, in much the same way as a film director directs actors, the engineer's prime responsibility is to record performances. Later, he or she has to mix them into a balanced final stereo **master**. Bands often build up strong relationships with their own sound engineer and use them in the studio as well as for live performances.

The sound engineer listens to the band from within the control room. By altering the settings on the mixing desk they can fine tune the recording.

On the job

Most sound engineers gain experience by working in a studio and some just learn on the job. They may go straight into the studio from school and use 'downtime' – when they are not actually working – to play around and learn skills on the **mixing** desk. Others take courses in sound engineering or music and sound recording. A good theoretical knowledge is important to help analyse the sounds heard in the studio, but work experience in the studio is absolutely vital. Sound engineers need a good ear for music and sounds generally, an understanding of the technical side of recording and a lot of patience!

The session

The composition of the band, and the type of music it plays, influence the way in which its music is recorded. The band can all be recorded together, or separately using **overdubbing**.

*Lesser-known bands may spend about twenty days recording and a further ten days **mixing**. However, major rock or pop bands could expect to be in the studio on and off for at least five months, three months of which will be solid recording. Seen here in the studio is country singer Garth Brooks.*

Laying the tracks

Let us assume that the band comprises drums, bass, rhythm guitar, lead guitar, keyboards and a singer. It is possible to record the band's performance as if 'live', in other words, straight on to tape with no subsequent additions or changes. However, it is more likely that the band would all perform together, but the **producer** would pay particular attention to the drums and may in fact only record them and nothing else. As long as the drums are recorded from one end of the song to the other, and played well, then everything else can be done as 'overdubs'. The drum provides the steady beat like a metronome. Overdubbing happens when a performer listens on headphones to instruments previously recorded on the **multi-track** whilst performing his or her own part simultaneously. Once the main instruments have been overdubbed, the lead vocal and backing vocals can follow on the same basis. It's even possible for a band to record a complete **track** without ever meeting each other at the studio. Each member's contribution can be recorded separately.

Getting it right

A **session** traditionally lasts three hours. In reality, little can be accomplished in that time so most sessions last a full day. Bands are expected to have rehearsed their songs before coming to the studio, so that they don't waste valuable studio time getting it right. Even so, they can expect to play the songs several times before any recording starts, so that the **sound engineer** is able to get the mix right.

On the job

Many solo artists rely on high-quality **session musicians** to play the instruments that feature on their backing tracks. A session musician is somebody who is hired to play a particular instrument on one or more of the tracks on an **album**. They are not regular members of the band. These musicians must be very adaptable and able to play in the style of the band. They are paid by the session and do not usually receive **royalties**. Sometimes, well-known musicians, particularly guitarists, make guest 'appearances' on tracks of other band's albums, for example Brian May of Queen and Eric Clapton.

Solo artists, such as Sheryl Crow, rely on session musicians to provide the backing tracks to their albums. A good session musician will be much in demand and can earn a good living.

Mixing the tracks

Once the **producer** is happy with everything recorded on the **multi-track**, the 'mix' can begin. This is the process of balancing and fine-tuning each individual sound on the multi-track and combining them through the **mixing** desk to make one final stereo combination, called the **master**.

Getting the right mix

Mixing is a very important part of the sound recording process. Some bands, perhaps in particular blues bands, can make a finished product from a fairly simple recording, and it will sound much like a live **session**. However, many pop **albums** rely on studio effects. These are the sounds made by the 'outboard gear' – the sound effect equipment – which can add echo or reverberation to sounds or control the maximum level of any one sound. For these albums the production in the studio is as important as the recorded sound itself.

Nowadays, it is possible for a sound engineer working on a digital mixing desk to alter the sound quite significantly from that which was recorded. The cleaning up of the sound and the addition of sound effects can all take place post-recording.

Recording techniques have changed so much in recent years that bands are often loathe to release previously unreleased material. The quality may be poor compared to the highly mixed albums of today and it may damage their reputation. However, when the **tracks** on Beatles albums such as *Sgt. Pepper's Lonely Hearts Club Band* are heard 'unmixed', it is obvious how good they were even before mixing.

Shaping the sound

With a 24-track mixing desk, some instruments and the vocals will be on an individual track, but the drums could be on lots of tracks. The guitar may be on two tracks, as there may be one microphone on the guitar and one ambient microphone that picks up the sounds in the room. These two tracks are then 'balanced' on the mix to get a good blend. When mixing, the **sound engineer** 'shapes' the sound by removing those parts that are not making a positive contribution, in order to get a cleaner, punchier sound.

Studio recording versus live recording

The best sound quality is achieved when a band records its music in the studio. However, many famous bands bring out albums made from live performances. In this case, the stage will be the 'playing area' and the 'control room' will be in a van outside the stage area. The van is set up as a mini-studio, but there are obvious disadvantages as the engineers cannot see the performers, except on closed circuit TV, and have no way of communicating with them. There is no opportunity for a second chance with a song as it is part of a live performance. However, there is the possibility of limited mixing of the tape afterwards in the studio.

The Spice Girls performing live. Live recordings may not have the sound quality of a studio recording, but they convey some of the excitement and spontaneity that members of the audience experience at a concert.

Technical tips

The mixing desk is covered with knobs, buttons and faders which adjust the sounds going through it. For example, some adjust the treble and bass sounds. Sounds are either routed to 24 individual tracks on a multi-track recorder or sent to hard disc recorders. These are computer-based systems that convert the incoming sounds into audio tracks in **digital** format before storing them. Although digital formats are becoming more popular, many prestigious studios prefer the old recording techniques, using tapes, as they consider that they produce better-sounding recordings.

Synthesized music

Many instruments played in pop and rock music today are electric or electronic instruments. The development of electronic music since the beginning of the 20th century has opened up a new world of sound. Individual instruments can now produce sounds that are louder and of a greater variety than ever before. Some musicians even create music in a recording studio that cannot be played live in a concert.

Today, electronic music is such a familiar sound to us that we do not always realize that we are not hearing actual instruments playing. Many musicians have experimented with the new possibilities presented by electronic equipment. Strange and exotic sounds can be produced by recording sounds on tape machines, then speeding them up and slowing them down, recording one sound on top of another or even playing sounds in reverse! It is perfectly possible to lay down drums, bass, strings and either guitar or keyboard live on a four-track recording machine, then record voice or an instrumental **track** over it **digitally** on a computer, without ever going into a recording studio.

An instrument called a theremin was the forerunner of the modern-day synthesizer. The theremin consisted of electronic circuits that produced weird, unearthly noises, completely unlike any other instrument. Here it is being used by the John Spencer Blues Explosion.

Much of the music played by DJs in clubs is produced on synthesizers. These recreate the sounds of many instruments, as well producing sound effects that would not be possible using conventional instruments. This style of music is much cheaper to produce as musicians are not required.

Synthesizers

The term '**synthesizer**' is the specific name for an electronic keyboard that reproduces the sounds of other instruments. Synthesizers can also make sounds that no ordinary instrument can make, by manufacturing new sound patterns. Modern, computerized synthesizers can **sample** sounds, which can then be stored in the memory. A collection of samples can then be built up. Sequencers in a synthesizer are designed to remember notes so, if a group of notes is played on the synthesizer, the sequencer will memorize it. The sequencer will then play back this musical phrase as many times as required. Nowadays, many musicians use sequencers to make backing tracks. When attached to a PC with music software, the synthesizer becomes a powerful tool for composers who can write their own music and perform it electronically using their computer. The software is used in much the same way as a **mixing** desk, altering and enhancing the sound.

Drum machines are the electronic equivalent of a drum set. They either produce a drum-like sound electronically or use sounds sampled from real drums. When the pad is hit with a stick, it produces an electronic signal that makes a drum sound. In disco and club music, where a precise, unchanging beat is needed, drum machines are particularly useful. Once a rhythm pattern has been fed into the drum machine, the sequencer can memorize the pattern and repeat it perfectly over and over again.

Young musicians can now use their PCs, electronic keyboards and synthesizers to produce good-quality **demo CDs** in their own homes, so avoiding the expense of hiring a studio.

Selecting the tracks

When a record company signs up a new band, it may not initially want to commit itself to financing an entire **album**. It may prefer to release a couple of **singles** first and, if these are successful, it may reserve the right to ask for further **tracks** to make an album. This is what some people refer to as a 'singles deal'.

The **advances** offered for a singles deal are not great and bands are often very unhappy with the commitment to produce a number of singles in a short time period. However, if the record company is not tying the band to it for ever, and things do not work out, the band can move on and hope for a more successful career elsewhere. On the other hand, if the singles are a success, the band will be in a very strong position to negotiate a full recording **contract**.

In the following contract period, the recording commitment will usually require a band to record sufficient tracks to make an album. This is usually between eight and twelve tracks. For the band, the fewer tracks the better because this makes it easier to satisfy the recording commitment and also because it helps to keep the recording costs down.

*A large number of singles are released each week. Singles are normally located near the front of shops, together with a **chart** listing, so that shoppers see them as they enter. Successful sales of a single may lead to the artist being offered an album deal.*

Often, a new band has to give the record company absolute control over the content of the album. Therefore, the band has to discuss this possible issue with the **A&R** department before signing a deal. Some bands have been caught out by record companies that have a commercial interest in a particular area of music, and insist that the band records certain types of songs.

George Michael was in dispute with his record company because he felt it was restricting his artistic development. He sued and lost in court and finally had to agree to a settlement before he was allowed to sign to another record company.

Greatest hits and compilations

Once a band has become really successful and released several albums, there comes the opportunity to release an album of 'greatest hits'. Also, compilation albums may be made of several different artists who play similar types of music. This provides another source of revenue from **royalties** as well as more exposure.

Making the video

The record company now has a **CD** with up to a dozen or so **tracks** of a band's music. However, today's audiences expect an audio-visual package – it is the age of the video and increasingly the **DVD**. It was not always like this. Back in 1975, when Queen released their **chart**-topping **single** 'Bohemian Rhapsody', it was promoted by the first-ever promotional music video.

Queen spent many months preparing A Night at the Opera, *one of the most extravagant and expensive* **albums** *of the era. They released 'Bohemian Rhapsody' as a pilot single that remained at number one in the UK charts for nine weeks. Its style was mock opera and it was promoted by the first-ever music video.*

Is a video really needed?

The amount of money spent on making a video depends on a number of factors, of which the primary one is 'What is it going to be used for?'. Many bands produce a promotional (promo) video to send to **promoters**, the **A&R** department at a record company or even TV **producers**. This is usually a video of a live performance and only costs a few thousand pounds. However, quality videos for broadcasting cost much more, so bands normally wait until they actually have a record deal. Then it is the record company who will fund the product for promotional purposes.

Video has the ability to capture the image of the band and the music at the same time, and this is why it is such a good promotional tool. Unless it is professionally made, with the right skill and budget, it could turn out badly edited or pretentious and be a very poor advertisement for the band. The best advice for a band just starting out is to make either a multi-camera recording of a live show, or a promo video that includes at least some footage of the band miming a 'live' performance. There is no need to add lots of special effects as these may draw more attention to the director than the band!

It is debatable whether a brilliant video can turn a second-rate record into a hit or not. However, video is now an accepted and almost essential medium in the hit-making process. Not long ago, videos were only for the top artists, but now they are expected for every record release and often for **demos** and even bookings.

Keeping control

Bands have to take care that they do not lose artistic control to the record company or management company who are financing the video. Big-name video directors are very expensive and have a huge production team, but they are not necessarily the best for every band, either commercially or artistically. Young directors may lack experience, but are likely to be full of new ideas that may project a new band's modern image better.

Promotional videos are an essential part of the marketing strategy. Record companies supply copies of the videos to record stores so that they can be played in-store. Market research has found that actually seeing the artist perform the single can boost sales.

Burning the CD

The CD factory

Now that the **tracks** are recorded and the video filmed, it's time to start producing the **CDs**. The first step in the manufacture of CDs is the production of a **master** disc or template from which all the others will be copied. The CD factory needs to be supplied with the music on Exabyte cassette, CD-R disc or Sony 1630 tape cassette prepared by a mastering studio.

Making the template

The template is made in a completely clean room with a safe yellow light. It is created by writing the **digital** data on to a glass master disc, using a **laser** that traces a spiral path on the surface of the spinning glass disc. The laser burns tiny indentations in the photosensitive coating, creating microscopic pits in the glass surface. This glass master is coated with a thin layer of nickel. Then the nickel layer is peeled off and trimmed to form the father **stamper** or master template.

Multiple copies

Polycarbonate crystals are melted and injection-moulded against the father stamper, producing a transparent disc with the data pattern stamped into the top side. This surface is protected by a thin layer of aluminium and a layer of **UV-curable** lacquer. The disc is then screen-printed and is ready for packaging. When the disc is inserted into a CD player, the data is read from the underside with the polycarbonate acting as a lens and the aluminium layer acting as a reflector.

Storing the digital information

Digital information is simply a series of numbers and, on a CD, these numbers are stored in a **binary** format. The pits on the surface of the CD represent 'one' while the gaps between the pits represent 'zero'. The pits are very small, just half a micron (one millionth of a metre) wide, and they are arranged in a thin spiral, starting at the centre of the disc. The width of this spiral track is just one-thirtieth the width of a human hair. This means that a vast amount of information can be stored on a CD – more than five thousand million bits.

Technical tips

The CD is read by a weaker laser than that which was used to burn the CD. As the laser beam passes across the surface of the CD, light is reflected from the shiny aluminium surface, but not from the pits. Hence the reflected beam is switched on and off in the same digital pattern as the pits. The pattern of the pits forms a stream of signals which are converted back into sound-waves and reproduced by the CD player.

(a)

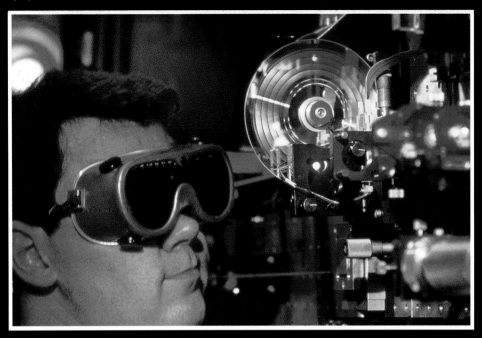

(b)

(a) *A worker checks the position of the glass master before switching on the laser. The glass master is twice the size of a standard CD and is coated in a light-sensitive material. The laser burns a series of pits on the surface of the master.*

(b) *Unlike **vinyl** LPs, copy CDs are moulded rather than pressed. This worker is operating the computer-controlled plastic moulding equipment which makes the CDs.*

Packaging

The design of the packaging is crucial for sales. Great packaging can sell poor music, but great music is unlikely to sell well in poor packaging.

Music **CDs** are usually packaged in a protective plastic or card **jewel case**. Inserted within the jewel case is a leaflet, the cover of which forms the cover of the CD. The small size of the jewel case allows shops to stack a large number of CDs either on shelves or in bins and makes it easy for the customer to flick through the CDs.

Getting the design right

A design team is **commissioned** to design the contents of the jewel case and the screen-print on the disc itself. The small size of the CD limits the amount of information that can be displayed on the cover, hence it is important that the cover is as eye-catching as possible. Designers also have to remember that CD catalogues and on-line music shops show the front of the CD as a tiny thumbnail image, making it difficult for the customer to see any detail on the cover.

The record company, together with the band, liaises with the design team to agree on the concept for the cover. Often the band has photographs specially taken for the cover and the back of the CD.

The designer may look through hundreds of photographs to find the one which will work well with the cover design. Often they look for a photo that has space either at the top, side or bottom where they can place the titles without obscuring the main subject of the photo.

The information printed within the leaflet usually includes the **lyrics** to the songs, credits and other information that the band think is relevant. There is an insert that slips under the back plastic of the jewel case, which is folded at each end to form the spine. This is where the title of the CD is printed so it can be read when the CD is stacked on a shelf. The back of the CD usually lists the songs that are on the **album**, together with **run-times** and **copyright** notices.

Buying on impulse

Many customers have never heard the music on the album. Their decision to buy may be based solely on what they have read about the album, or on the appearance of the cover. Researchers who watch how customers flick through piles of CDs have discovered that the decision to buy can be made in just a couple of seconds. Designers may be tempted to reduce the size of the text so that more can be fitted on, but research shows that people like to be able to read the information on the covers easily, especially the title, the name of the group and the contents.

Sometimes, a record company will release a limited edition of the album that is priced higher than the normal one. Often it consists of a jewel case that is inserted inside an outer sleeve. Packaged inside will be additional information, folded posters or promotional photocards.

Often, the most effective cover designs involve the use of distinctive graphics which are easily recognisable, such as that on Tubular Bells *(top left) or* The Division Bell *(bottom centre). One of simplest album designs was the plain white cover of The Beatles'* White Album.

On the job

Graphic designers produce the artwork which is used on CD covers. Most use software programmes to produce the artwork which can be a combination of illustrations and photographs. Most graphic designers have taken courses at art colleges or universities. They need to be creative people who can work well with other people in the design team and are able to interpret the wishes of the client.

Other media

If you go inside a music shop to buy an **album**, you have an amazing selection of different types of media to choose from. The most popular format is the **CD**. However, the record companies know that some people prefer different formats to the CD or are still using older equipment, so it is possible to buy the same album on **vinyl**, cassette, **DVD**, **mini-disc** and on a music video.

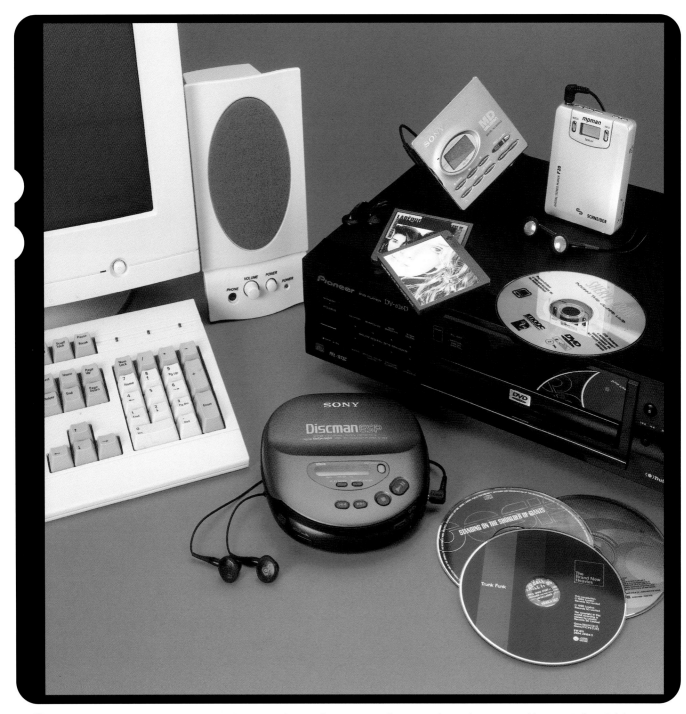

Nowadays, people can listen to music everywhere they go, making use of portable CD, mini-disc and MP3 players. Music can also be played back through the speakers on a computer.

What is a DVD?

DVD (**digital** versatile – or video – disc) is a format for storing data that can hold four to eight times more than a CD. It was developed primarily for digital movies which could be played on a television, and there is already a wide variety of rock, pop and classical concert videos available on DVD. However, although a DVD standard for audio only (called DVD-Audio) is under development, this was not finalized at the time of writing. The main improvement that DVD offers over CD, apart from the increase in capacity, is the ability to store audio coded in Dolby Digital and other 'Surround Sound' formats. When played through the five or six speakers that are necessary, the effect is far superior to the simple stereo available on CDs. In fact, it is just like being present in a concert hall.

Mini-discs

The mini-disc was developed by Sony and first appeared in the shops in 1992. It measures just 7 cm by 7 cm and holds 74 minutes of music. The mini-disc was designed to be a cheap, portable digital recording medium with near CD quality, which could compete with the cassette. There are two forms of mini-disc; conventional pre-mastered discs and recordable discs (or blanks). The recordable mini-disc has many advantages over both the CD-R (recordable CD) and the cassette tape. Once the music has been recorded, the **tracks** can be reordered or erased. In fact, mini-discs can be recorded and erased thousands of times without any loss in quality, unlike cassette tapes. They come in a hard plastic case which protects them from scratching. Mini-disc players have a shock resistant memory which means that the audio is not affected by movement and bumps if the player is worn while jogging, for example. The mini-disc is relatively expensive and has been slow to take off, but it is gaining in popularity in Japan and Europe.

MP3

The latest 'buzz-word' is MP3, which is a means of compressing digital audio so that it occupies very much less storage space. This compression does have a drawback, for while it is possible to compress a CD from approximately 650MB down to around 60MB or less, the sound quality is poorer when played back. However, compression of this order means that it is now possible to **download** music of reasonable quality from the Internet. There are already hundreds of MP3 music sites on the Internet, and 'MP3' is currently the most searched-for word on many Internet search engines. Many sites allow users to download **sample** tracks for free to give them a taste of the album. If they like what they hear, they can order the CD or download the whole album once payment has been made. It takes about three minutes to download a single track, which can then be stored on the computer and replayed or burnt on to a CD. Files can also be downloaded into the temporary memory of portable MP3 players. Some bands are now producing albums that are only available in MP3 format via the Internet.

Digital problems

It is estimated that within the next three years, 30 per cent of all music will be acquired digitally. The illegal copying of music CDs and tapes is already a big problem in the music industry. The ease with which MP3 tracks can be downloaded, copied and passed from computer to computer will make it much worse. New technologies such as electronic watermarking will be essential to stop people downloading music and making multiple copies for their friends.

Making a Hit

The release!

The band has made its **album** at last! The **CD** is going to be released, but this is not the end of the story. It is now that all the hard work associated with promoting the record begins.

On the road

Now is the time to promote the band by touring at home and abroad. At this stage, the **manager** will employ a tour manager to look after the band whilst it is on tour.

A major tour will employ many people. A well-known rock band on a European tour, playing a different venue most nights, will need a crew of at least 30 people and probably a fleet of vehicles! As well as the tour manager, there will be a team of 'roadies' who move the truckloads of kit into the venue, set up the stage and then repack it afterwards. Also needed are **sound engineers**, personal assistants and even caterers. Tours are expensive and they frequently lose money. Bands can pay to join a better-known band on tour as a support act. This way they get to play to a larger audience than they could if they were on their own.

A stressful time

A tour provides an opportunity for the band members to spend time together, working on their live act, adding new arrangements and writing new material. However, it can also be a time of great stress. Bands have to endure a gruelling schedule – playing in different towns or even countries night after night. The itinerary opposite, for Britney Spears' 2000 tour, shows just how relentless this schedule can be. Musicians say that there is often no opportunity for a proper night's sleep and eating is frequently just a fast food snack grabbed whenever the opportunity arises. Sleep deprivation and exhaustion can lead to frayed nerves and it can become difficult for the band members to get along well together. They are used to spending a lot of time together rehearsing and performing, but it is a different matter living in close proximity day after day.

On the job

A tour manager will arrange passports, visas and work permits, transport, equipment hire, insurance, accommodation, the fee and much more. Anyone who has managed a band on the road will be able to tell stories of lost passports, missing band members, theft of equipment, missed planes due to misprinted itineraries, **contracts** not being honoured and food or drink not provided in the dressing room, breakdown of transport and so on! You may begin to wonder why anyone goes on tour, but of course it is not only essential for publicity and money, it can be great fun!

Tour Itinerary for Britney Spears
June–November 2000

20 June	Columbia, Maryland
21 June	Hartford, Connecticut
23 June	New York
24 June	Hershey, Pennsylvania
25 June	Scranton, Pennsylvania
27–30 June	Wantagh, New York
2–3 July	Holmdel, New Jersey
4 July	Bristow, Virginia
5 July	Camden, New Jersey
7 July	Tinley Park, Illinois
8 July	Milwaukee, Wisconsin
9 July	Clarkston, Michigan
16 July	Maryland Heights, Missouri
17 July	Bonner Springs, Kansas
19 July	Dallas, Texas
20 July	San Antonio, Texas
21–22	Woodlands, Texas
26 July	Denver, Colorado
27 July	Albuquerque, New Mexico
28 July	Phoenix, Arizona
29 July	Irvine, California
30–31 July	Los Angeles, California
1 Aug	Concord, California
3 Aug	San Diego, California
4 Aug	Las Vegas, Nevada
5 Aug	San Bernardino, California
6 Aug	Marysville, California
8 Aug	Mountain View, California
10 Aug	Portland, Oregon
11 Aug	George, Washington
12 Aug	Vancouver, BC, Canada
14 Aug	Salt Lake City, Utah
21 Aug	Burgettstown, Pennsylvania
22 Aug	Toronto, ON, Canada
23 Aug	Montreal, QC, Canada
24 Aug	Syracuse, New York
25 Aug	Atlantic City, New Jersey
28 Aug	Mansfield, Massachusetts
30 Aug	Saratoga Springs, New York
31 Aug	Cleveland, Ohio
1 Sept	Knoxville, Tennessee
2 Sept	Noblesville, Indiana
3 Sept	Columbus, Ohio
9 Sept	Orlando, Florida
10 Sept	West Palm Beach, Florida
12 Sept	Raleigh, North Carolina
13 Sept	Charlotte, North Carolina
14 Sept	Virginia Beach, Virginia
15 Sept	Burgettstown, Pennsylvania
17 Sept	Antioch, Tennessee
18 Sept	Atlanta, Georgia
20 Sept	New Orleans, Louisiana
7–8 Oct	Birmingham, UK
10–12 Oct	Wembley Arena, London
13–14 Oct	Manchester, UK
17 Oct	Bielefeld, Germany
18 Oct	Gent, Belgium
19 Oct	Dortmund, Germany
20 Oct	Stuttgart, Germany
22 Oct	Barcelona, Spain
24 Oct	Milan, Italy
25 Oct	Zurich, Switzerland
26 Oct	Munich, Germany
28 Oct	Kiel, Germany
29 Oct	Berlin, Germany
30 Oct	Hannover, Germany
1 Nov	Leipzig, Germany
2 Nov	Frankfurt, Germany
4 Nov	Arnhem, Holland
7 Nov	Gothenburg, Sweden
8 Nov	Oslo, Norway
9 Nov	Stockholm, Sweden
10 Nov	Copenhagen, Denmark
11 Nov	Wetten TV Studio
13 Nov	Koln, Germany
14 Nov	Paris, France

*A few of the many cases that have to be moved from **gig** to gig. All of the equipment has to be carefully packed away in hard-sided cases so that it is not damaged during transit.*

Promoting the tracks

Getting on the playlist of a major radio station is critical to success. Although the playlist is selected by the producers of the shows, DJs can influence record sales by being enthusiastic about certain singles.

The **album** may be the best ever produced, but it will not sell unless it gets into the public eye. Everything has to be done simultaneously as there is little point in bringing the public's attention to the album when they cannot buy it anywhere. Reviews and copies of the **CD** must be sent to the national press. Then, at the same time as everyone hears about the release, the major distribution companies must get the album into the music stores.

Plugging through the media

The new release has to be promoted by advertising, radio airplay, TV appearances, newspaper articles, magazine interviews and even publicity stunts!

The vast majority of **singles** become hits through exposure on national radio and TV. Regular appearances on either almost guarantee **chart** success. There is fierce competition to get on **playlists** and even more for coveted performances on TV music programmes. Nowadays, with so many satellite TV channels, it is possible to obtain world-wide TV coverage. A playlist is a list of records that will be played a guaranteed number of times per week by a radio station. The records are chosen by a small panel of radio **producers** and put into categories, with records by less well-known bands starting off in a lower rotation so the producers can watch and wait to see how they progress. Only major artists can expect to land an 'A' listing from the release date. It is the producers who choose the playlists, not the DJs, so it is the producers whom the pluggers approach with the release. Pluggers are people who are employed to get records and videos played, using their network of contacts in the industry.

There is a wide range of magazines which cover the comings and goings in the music industry. Managers will work with the magazine editor to make sure that their band is featured in the magazine, and if possible, on the cover.

The charts

Charts are lists of best-selling singles and albums, which are put together by market research companies. Nowadays, there are many different charts, such as Indie, Soul and Metal, but national radio stations and top TV programmes use the Gallup Chart. This is a chart produced by a company that has a network of hundreds of shops around the country (chart return shops). These have special computers to log the catalogue number of every record sold. It takes about 7000 sales a week to get into the Top 40. A chart-topping single will make up to 200,000 sales. The MRIB chart is favoured by other radio and TV stations as well as many national newspapers. This chart is not just sales-based. A panel of expert observers takes into account sales, radio play, live performances and so on, and there is therefore less chance of any fiddling of sales figures.

In the USA, the Top 100 singles, Top 200 albums and related charts are published in *Billboard Magazine*. These charts take sales and radio plays into account. In Australia, the Australian Record Industry Association (ARIA) produces singles and album charts based on sales.

Merchandising

The band can also be promoted by selling such items as T-shirts, baseball caps, badges, key-rings and posters to fans. Selling these at performances is fun, the fans love them, they provide extra finance and are a very good advertisement for the band.

Merchandising is an important source of income for successful bands. At the top level of merchandising, companies work on a basis similar to that of record companies. The band is paid an **advance** for their merchandising rights and receives a **royalty** payment when this advance has been recouped. This involves substantial financial risk on the part of the merchandising company, so it has to be very sure that the image is a saleable commodity.

What are the costs?

The costs of making **singles** and **albums** for release are high. A debut single can cost upwards of £5000 and that does not include packaging, marketing and making the promotional video. The production costs of an album can amount to hundreds of thousands of pounds.

Britney Spears is one of the most successful teenage artists of recent years. Her revenue from singles and albums is supplemented by income from videos, personal appearances and merchandising.

The record companies do not actually pay for the costs of recording. They **advance** the band enough money to make the single and then they recover these costs from the sales of the single. The **producer** is usually given an advance paid for by the record company. This is then treated as part of the recording costs. The band will not receive any more money until the single has broken even, in other words until the production costs have been covered by the income from sales. Obviously, the lower the recording costs, the fewer the **CDs** that have to be sold in order to break even.

When does a band start to make money?

An amazing number of expenses have to be met before a band receives any money. Most bands are offered a **royalty** deal that is a percentage of the retail value of the CD (the price of the CD in the shops). The usual figure is about eight per cent of the retail price, less VAT and certain other deductions. All royalties have to be split between the band members. Fortunately, royalties are payable for the whole period of **copyright** of the album, which is 50 years. There are many well-known singles that are still selling years after they were first released, earning their creators a steady income.

So let us take a theoretical example. Imagine a band was advanced £250,000 to record an album. Out of this advance, the band has to pay for the recording studio, any special equipment, the producer and **sound engineer**, the **mixing** costs and many other related costs. Remember, too, that the band members will have to live on this money until their album starts selling in the shops and the advance is paid off. During this time they will have to supplement their income by doing **gigs** and going on tour. The record company will also want to recover the costs of photography sessions, showcases, advertising, travelling expenses, **promoters** and touring, and half of the promotional video costs.

Only a fraction of the money raised from selling an album will reach the band. Bands need to sell hundreds of thousands of albums in order to pay off their advances and start earning a living.

The retail prices of CD albums in a shop are quite high, but the band will only earn a fraction of these costs. On average, a full-priced album will earn the band £80,000 from 100,000 sales. However, there will be further deductions for packaging costs, which can add up to 25 per cent of the royalties. This means that approximately 500,000 albums need to be sold before the advance is paid off and the band starts making money. The band will receive a performing royalty every time its recording is played on radio or TV.

Songwriters receive royalties from all the sales and performances of their songs via their **publisher**. Sales of singles and albums generate record royalties or 'mechanicals'. For each record sold, the record companies pay the publisher a royalty. This works out at approximately five pence per **track**. Also, songwriters receive a share of the performing royalties from radio broadcasts and TV. Therefore, if a songwriter is a member of the band, he or she will earn more money than the other members.

Handling new-found wealth

Many successful young musicians can amass enormous wealth, out of all proportion to their age. These people need financial advice so that they use their fortune wisely. Strong, supportive family and friends can also help the band to keep their feet firmly on the ground. It is expensive to make **demos**, albums, videos, buy band equipment and so on, therefore money earned should be used wisely. Many successful musicians have squandered their millions on an extravagant lifestyle, only to find that 20 years later they have nothing left. It is a similar scenario to that of lottery winners, who imagine that suddenly owning millions will bring them happiness, and find instead that their lives are destroyed.

Staying successful

It is one thing to be able to write a hit song, but can the band continue to produce top quality material every year for their fans? During the seven-year life of The Beatles, they released twelve **albums** – one or two per year – with twenty-two **chart**-topping **singles**. In contrast, Oasis have made four albums over the last six years. Often, artists find it necessary to change their style to stay current. For example, in recent years, older artists such as Cher and Tom Jones have revamped their old songs, recorded with younger artists and as a result have made chart-topping songs.

Cher is one of many artists of the 1960s and 1970s who are seeing a surge in their popularity due to the current sensation known as 'retro-cult'.

There are pressures in staying together as a band. Members spend long hours together and this puts a strain on relationships. Issues such as credits, **royalty** payments and choice of **tracks** for compilation albums have all caused rifts in groups. Lead singers tend to attract more attention than drummers and bass players and this too can cause disharmony. Sometimes, female members have been found to be paid less money than their male counterparts, as was recently revealed in the group Steps. When bands split up, members are faced with the choice of going solo or finding a new career path. A few band members have gone on to have successful solo careers, such as Robbie Williams once of Take That and George Michael of Wham!. The four members of the Spice Girls have managed to record both as a group and as individual artists simultaneously, with mixed success.

The Internet future

Developments in the Internet are forcing the music industry to change. At the moment, the **CD** is the main delivery medium, but more and more people are **downloading** music straight from the Internet.

The Internet is creating opportunities for independent **labels** and individual bands. Young musicians are finding that they can reach their audience without the need for **agents**, **promoter**s and record companies. They can set up their own website and let people download their music. Their live **gigs** can also be played over the Internet, reaching millions of people. It is difficult to predict whether songwriters of the future will need the services of a music **publisher**. However, it is possible that protecting **copyrights** will become even more difficult and the role of the music publisher in collecting royalties could become increasingly important.

Some Internet companies will offer the consumer the opportunity to put together their own favourite compilations and download them. However, many people will still prefer to browse through CDs at their local music store.

The two Live Aid concerts held simultaneously in London and New York in 1985 were seen by millions around the world. The money raised was used to help the famine victims of drought-stricken Africa.

The music industry has seen so much change over the last few years that it is impossible to predict exactly what the future will hold for musicians. However, one thing is clear – the industry will continue to grow, giving consumers an even greater choice of music.

Using fame to help others

One positive phenomenon that has occurred in recent times is the way that the most successful names in the music world are using their fame and resources to support the work of charities around the world. Examples of this are events like Band Aid, Live Aid and the various AIDS Benefit concerts of the 1980s. The organizers of such huge events were people like Bob Geldof (from the Boomtown Rats), Peter Gabriel (from Genesis), and Sting (from Police). They took advantage of the fact that they had a vast following of fans who would support massive musical events in aid of deserving charities.

Glossary

A&R   stands for Artists and Repertoire. They are people in a record company who listen to demo CDs and decide which artists to sign up.

advance   money paid before it is due. For example, a record company gives a band enough money to make a single and then recovers the money from sales of the single.

agent   person who arranges live performances and tours for artists

album   collection of songs released together on one CD or record

binary   numbering system involving two digits, 0 and 1

CD   stands for compact disc, a disc on which a large amount of digital information can be stored

chart   lists of the best-selling singles and albums; there are many types of chart, each listing a particular type of music

commission   fee paid to an agent or designer, for example, for services such as selling goods or creating CD covers

contract   legal agreement made between two or more people

copyright   exclusive legal right given to an author, songwriter or artist to publish and perform original material for a specified period of time

demo   short for demonstration, a CD containing a few songs by an aspiring band

digital   information in the form of a series of binary digits (1 and 0) that are the building blocks of computer technology

download   to copy a file from one computer to another, typically from a web server to your own

DVD   stands for digital versatile – or video – disc, a format for storing data that can hold four to eight times more than a CD

feedback   return of the output signal from the amplifier

gig   performance or concert

jam   improvised playing of instruments by a group of musicians

jewel case   plastic container that contains a CD

label   name or trademark under which a small, independent recording company trades or a division of a larger recording company operates

laser   piece of equipment that produces an intense beam of light. A powerful laser beam is used to make the pits on the surface of a CD.

lyrics   words of a song

manager   person who is responsible for the business concerns of an artist

master   high-quality finished recording that is copied on to CDs for duplication

mini-disc   very small compact disc for storing digital information

mixing   making adjustments to a music recording to improve the quality of the sound

multi-track   having many tracks, or being able to record many different tracks on the same piece of tape

overdub   to record sounds on to an existing recording

playlist   songs that are selected to be played on a radio station

producer   person who is in overall control of the recording process and decides on the sounds he or she wants from the band

promoter   person or company who finances gigs and tours and books bands for venues

publisher   company that publishes music and is responsible for collecting all the money earned by songs and for protecting the copyright of songwriters

royalty   sum paid to an author, performer or songwriter for each book sold or each performance of a work

run-time   length of time a recording takes to play. A single is around three minutes long.

sample   to extract a (short) sound from a recording. Samples are recorded sounds placed in the memory of a synthesizer to be used at a future date.

sampler   the equipment that samples sound

session   period of time spent recording or jamming

session musician   musician who is not signed up to any one record company and who plays on sessions for various artists

single   one song that is released on its own, usually of three- to four-minute duration

sound engineer   person who is responsible for recording a performance in a recording studio and carrying out the mix to produce the final master

stamper   template that is produced in CD manufacture

synthesizer   electronic instrument, operated by a keyboard, that can produce a wide range of sounds

talent scout   person who is on the look-out for new bands. Scouts attend live gigs at clubs, pubs and small venues and will recommend a band to the A&R people.

track   one of several items recorded on a disc or tape, for example guitars and vocals. Track can also refer to a complete song.

UV-curable   describes a substance that hardens or cures when exposed to ultraviolet light

vinyl   type of plastic used to make records

Index